The Passive Business for Starters

What's Passive Income and How You Can Take Advantage of It

By: Donnie Pratt

9781681279565

Publishers Notes

Disclaimer – Speedy Publishing LLC

This publication is intended to provide helpful and informative material. It is not intended to diagnose, treat, cure, or prevent any health problem or condition, nor is intended to replace the advice of a physician. No action should be taken solely on the contents of this book. Always consult your physician or qualified health-care professional on any matters regarding your health and before adopting any suggestions in this book or drawing inferences from it.

The author and publisher specifically disclaim all responsibility for any liability, loss or risk, personal or otherwise, which is incurred as a consequence, directly or indirectly, from the use or application of any contents of this book.

Any and all product names referenced within this book are the trademarks of their respective owners. None of these owners have sponsored, authorized, endorsed, or approved this book.

Always read all information provided by the manufacturers 'product labels before using their products. The author and publisher are not responsible for claims made by manufacturers.

This book was originally printed before 2015. This is an adapted reprint by Speedy Publishing LLC with newly updated content designed to help readers with much more accurate and timely information and data.

Speedy Publishing LLC

40 E Main Street, Newark, Delaware, 19711

Contact Us: 1-888-248-4521

Website: http://www.speedypublishing.co

REPRINTED Paperback Edition: 9781681279565

Manufactured in the United States of America

Dedication

This book can provide information that every reader needs. That's why I dedicated this book to those who are determined to make good profit in Passive Income Business.

Table of Contents

Chapter 1- Understanding Passive Income 5

Chapter 2- What You Should Know About Passive Income 7

Chapter 3- Using Different Kinds of Passive Income 10

Chapter 4- How Can SEO Help Passive Income to Maximize Proportions 19

Chapter 6- Setting Goals and Having a Plan to Make More Money 21

Chapter 7- Easy and Quick Ways to Make Money Online 24

Chapter 8- Methods and Means for Passive Income Generation ... 35

Chapter 8- The Secret Methods of Using Passive Income Generators 40

Chapter 9- What You Should Know About Online and Offline Business 43

About The Author 46

Chapter 1 - Understanding Passive Income

There are currently some very popular and common ways to derive passive income. Writing a new melody or song or even a jingle and the selling it as a commercial property will garner some very lucrative passive income. Opening a bank savings account, is another way which just by saving money get the individual some interest residual income though it is not that much and fluctuates often at the whim and fancy of the banking systems.

Passive income is income generated repeatedly from doing something just ONCE! We can further define it as:

"Passive income is a revenue stream that you create that operates hours a day 7 seven days a week without any additional input. It can be considered an automatic ATM machine spitting out money every day. "

One example of a passive income stream would be an affiliate program. Yet another example would be ad revenue from ads on your website, or your blog. So massive passive income can best be described as generating greater than normal or considerable amounts of income from something you did just ONE time.

Staring a multi level business is another way to generate passive income. There are some multi level companies that don't require the standard work of recruiting and selling product but just to use their products. Becoming a financial product consultant is not only a good passive income source it is also a way to expand the client base.

For those with a little more money to spare, they can consider other type of investments which are likely to bring in the returns. Buying property and they letting it out helps the individual to pay for the loan thus not requiring any immediate financial commitment.

There are a lot of innovative ways to make money of the internet engine. All it takes is a little time spent to look for the legitimate business tools. One of the more popular tools include the creation of one's own information for e books and other sell on line tools that require perhaps language changes.

On the more risky way of getting passive income would be to invest in various stocks and bonds. However the risks levels are quite high and often not worth the risks.

Chapter 2 - What You Should Know About Passive Income

The "passive" part is misleading: There is always some focused work at the beginning, which can feel like a lot, to a new marketer. Sometimes, if you're really new, there is a sharp learning curve as you learn to operate the other necessary programs, methods or systems you need for your business. But it's well worth the effort to go that step further to creating passive income from as many sources as possible, because once you've set up your passive income plants, with just a little watering now and then, you really can make steady autopilot profit.

How much – and how labor intensive your efforts will have to be – depends on a number of factors.

Set Up as Many Sites as You Can

To put it into perspective, if you plant one tomato plant, that little plant might give off a bumper crop of tomatoes to eat at home – but 50 plants would give you enough to sell at a roadside stand. So it is with passive income: The more ventures you have working for you, the more income keeps flooding in.

Choose Particular Passive Income Method

Some are better than others at producing a high sales or profit yield – but no matter what method you decide on, there are actions you can take to dramatically increase the amount of income your chosen method is capable of generating for you. (And it s important to suit the method and the media to the campaign.)

Run an Affiliate Program

Running an affiliate program is not as daunting as it may sound. Later on, we'll show you an easy way to run an affiliate program with very little work. Affiliates sell your product to their list and each member in turn may sell it to his or her list... When you stop to think, it makes no sense to sell a product and not have affiliates to multiply those sales with their own lists!

Be Diligent About Tracking

It's no secret that the most lucrative forms of passive income benefit from regular tracking. This shouldn't be intimidating: There are many different tracking options, and we will discuss the most common in this report.

Decide to Use Paid Advertising

There is no doubt that using PPC (pay per click) advertising such as Google AdWords can significantly boost your passive income results. But is it the best strategy for new marketers?

Diversify

The old cliché: "Don't put all your eggs in one basket" is a good one, particularly when it comes to online passive income. But there's a fine line between diversifying, and overwhelming yourself with too many passive income sources in too many places.

Be Organized

It's crucial to be on top of your passive income empire, aware of what's going on with each "branch" – you can lose serious cash or opportunities by ignoring tracking, presenting offers to the wrong market, or assuming everything's running like clockwork. We're going to discuss solid methods for making sure unnecessary loss doesn't happen to you.

Accurately Do Your Keyword Research.

Research is one of the most important areas to "get right" – and even top marketers will tell you it is still "trial and error". But even though we're going to talk about keywords, there's an added level of depth to the subject of knowing your niche that we're about to thoroughly explore.

And, of course, whichever method(s) of online passive income you choose as your income-generating vehicle – you'll need to know how to drive traffic to your site.

Chapter 3- Using Different Kinds of Passive Income

Residual Income

After paying off all monthly commitments the money left over is known as residual income. This income can be of great help to an individual and is normally linked to the older more established income group. This is also the way the banking industry calculates the probability of giving out a loan commitment to their clients. This is an income that also continues to give well past the time frame of the first initial payment.

There are many ways to try and earn residual income. Writing for instance is one way of adventuring into this realm of gaining residual income.

If the writing material is good there would be a chance to sell the rights, and so it is with other avenues like writing a workable software program, composing a song, inventing a gadget and many more.

Like some famous actor and singer, where there are still payments coming in every time the work previously done is reused. When this is done for further entertainment modes, the said entertainer gets a residual income in the form of certain percentages form the original initial performance.

Earning residual income from real estate is perhaps one of the more popular styles of investment with this intention in mind. If done well this type of residual income in the most ideal and profitable.

Other much simpler ways of getting residual income would include starting a savings plan early on in age. Keeping to this diligently would help to ensure the comfortable retirement where residual income would be a great help.

The best types of residual income plans are normally where the individual had total autonomy over how, where and when the product is used. In being able to dictate the using methods the individual also has the end say over how the general promotion and other aspects of the invention go.

Leveraged Income

This is perhaps among the most beneficial ways of creating the possibility of having a continuous income in a long term scenario. Using the leverage income style, the individual ears more money with much less effort simply because the profits made don't only come as a direct result of one's own efforts but also from the added sources of other people's efforts.

Ideally most people work towards trying to earn this style of income both in the short term and long term scenario. In its most basic terms, leverage income allows the individual to concentrate on other endeavors once the initial stages of setting up and getting a particular project started. This said project is then left to generate income with no need for anymore particular daily involvements on the part of the investor or inventor.

Most people who are financially comfortable have ventured into this type of investment, with the intentions of generating some sort of leveraged income. Using a little time and effort to realize a project and then stepping back as the project eventually runs itself is indeed the perfect scenario. Thus this leverage style of earning power gives the individual the option to retire early and enjoy the fruits of his or her labor without the hassle of having to oversee the foray or having to be physically involved.

Besides the various investment arms that can be used to generate leveraged income, starting up a network marketing company or business venture is also another one of the more popular ways of generating this style of income. This of course requires a little hard work in the beginning but once the business is established then there will no longer be a need to be as completely involved as in the initial stages.

Active Leveraged Income

Active leveraged income works on more or less the same principals of the normal leverage income format with one significant distinction. In this style the individual will be required to be more hands on and have a higher percentage of involvement in the initial stage and at some stagnated stage throughout the foray.

Being able to provide a service or product that "keeps on giving" on a large scale would be of course quite ideal, thus making a study of such a product or service may bring about some rather interesting and viable options.

Some of the simple options of active leveraged income would include providing one's services at workshop conferences and seminars. Also conducting training session for corporations is also beneficial as the material used would have already been designed as a basic format to be used over and over again with only a few adjustments being made every so often.

Designing good home study modules are also another very profitable way of garnering the leveraged income style of earning a comfortable living. This also requires an initial investment of time and effort which usually create the platform for continuous and profitable sources of income. Thus by doing so, it allows the individual to then be able to focus on other possible forays to further enhance the income base.

The more successful formulas used in the past just required the individual to focus on designing a product or service that would be continuously and consistently used and reused, thus creating the desired revenue that would eventually evolve into leveraged income.

There are basically three types of leveraged income styles.

     1. The active leverage style

     2. The passive leverage style

     3. The basic leverage style.

All there style require some degree of initial work but if well designed and executed the long term hand on participation, it can be kept to a minimal level.

Using Internet Marketing

Internet marketing is also referred to by several other terms such as digital marketing, web marketing, online marketing, search marketing, and e marketing. All these have the similar marketing style with only a few minor difference but all have the main intention of making money.

This style of marketing is considered to be fairly broad and lucrative. This style may include services like creative and technical assistance, designing, development, advertising and sales. The various possible services the internet marketing tool can provide include the interactive customer engagement, a search engine provider for marketing purposes, a platform for ads, and many other possible earning tools.

The use of the internet marketing tool can provide for the one to one approach which is not always possible in the "real" world scenario. This approach though fairly broad and with no particular direction can be reached through the use of key words which are entered by the user in order to garner the required information or service.

Designing marketing tools which are supposed to appeal to specific interest groups is also done through the internet marketing route. This style created the platform for the connections to be made between a typical segment group and the product touted.

Niche marketing done through the internet marketing tool has its merits. The success of the style is very successful indeed and is certainly popular with those people who have limited time and interest to browse the internet. Thus this service provided is very beneficial to them and wide used too.

The advantages of creating an internet marketing business has it many advantages, ranging from the possible huge incomes derived to the leisure pace one can dictate. However nothing of course comes without some level of effort put in to see the success desired and being the most common tool of business now, it is well worth the effort to look into.

Network Marketing

It is a people person form of marketing, there is an actual need for people to go out and look for customers who may be interested in the products being sold. This method is used when it is deemed better than garnering any business through other methods like off line and on line marketing tools. Here the use of independent representatives is the key to the success rate of the business foray.

Recruitment drives are often conducted to try to get people to sign on to be agents or individual promoters for a company. Some of these companies follow the multi level marketing styles while others just need to identify potential distributors.

Using the network marketing to create residual income is another form of providing for a more comfortable living from a financial angle. This form of earning is done at the individual own pace and commitment. Basically the harder one works the better the chances will be to gain a higher residual income. The individual also has the privilege of deciding who and when to conduct any business with. This is a very important aspect for some people who enjoy meeting and making new friends while at the same time gaining the advantage of an extra income source.

This method also usually involves very little monetary investment and neither does it involve a long term commitment. The reason most people opt to try their hand at network marketing is because of the very lucrative promise of a residual income prospect. Seeing the success of others who have managed to achieve a comfortable financial status is a good bench mark to focus on in the pursuit of the individual's own ambitions for a good and healthy residual income. Another interesting thing to note is that there is no age limit to this kind of endeavor.

Real Estate

This is another form of creating residual income without having to be too confined to any particular style or commitment requirement. Suing real estate to create residual income is fast gaining popularity as the success rate and remunerations can be rather enticing.

Some of the "pull" factors include the ability to control the levels achieved in terms of income garnered. There are very rarely any quotas that are put in place or forced upon the agents.

However for some real estate agents that who are attached to certain companies there are various incentive programs that are put in place to help generate the drive to push the agents to higher achievement standards.

Creating one's own personal security with the residual income from selling real estate is also another attractive reason to venture into this endeavor. The income that is derived from this particular type of residual income is definitely worth the reason for working towards an early retirement plan.

In making the decision to venture into the real estate style of garnering residual income the sense of being able to have some control over one's own priorities is an advantage. This will also allow the individual to practice a sense of responsibility and commitment in order to see the success of his or her foray into real estate.

There are also some very good tax advantages in using real estate to garner a tidy residual income base. This can be reflected in the system that is currently used to encourage the active sale of real estate. Thus by providing the necessary tax breaks the individual is more likely to work even harder to achieve a comfortable residual income target.

Diversifying one's ability to garner residual income without having the hassle of having to set up a separate company or organization is a better option to consider as the real estate foray really does not require these facilities.

Using Blogs

Using this method for the purpose of earning residual income is a need thing at the moment. For those who are internet savvy this is an excellent avenue to pursue in the venture of creating residual income for one's self.

Thought having a certain level of experience is somewhat necessary, it is not absolute as everyone has to start somewhere. Learning to use the best techniques available to create successful blogs will directly relate to the amount of residual income derived.

In order to be able to achieve a fairly lucrative residual income from blogging there must be a certain amount of commitment. The success of blogging depends largely on the individual's interest levels and ability to look for relevant information in order to ensure the blogs done are interesting and captivating.

Focusing on the promotional aspect of blogging will ensure the relevant amount of exposure needed to make the blog as frequently visited as possible. Promoting one's content on a social networking website and also leaving the relevant web page information will ensure the blog is well connected. This is also create the higher percentages required when there is more traffic generated via referral sites.

Featuring advertisements on the individual's blog will also provide a source of income as the individual is in the position to charge for the postings. This is only applicable if the traffic to the said blog site is a lot, thus there will be a lot of other people or companies willing to pay to be feature as adverts within the blog site, with the intention that it will in turn bring traffic to their sites too.

Getting other people to write interesting things that are then featured in the individual's own blog is a very good way to keep the blog interesting and diversified.

Chapter 4- How Can SEO Help Passive Income to Maximize Proportions

Another asset you will need, if you truly want to grow your passive income efforts to maximum proportions: Effective Search Engine Optimization.

Before your stomach starts to knot at the thought of delving into SEO, however, forget any ideas you might have involving complex algorithms, costly subscriptions, an ad budget that breaks your piggybank, clever manipulation of META-data, or hours of time.

SEO is really quite simple, and the only constant that seems to be in play this new decade is another paradox: SEO blog post complaints and forum posts all seem to be confirming that the more you attempt to artificially or even just intelligently boost yourself in Google's rankings, the less likely you are, these days, to succeed.

Today, more than ever, writing original content that speaks directly to your target subscriber is essential – but don't confuse original content with "clever" content. This has nothing to do with digging up statistically favorable long tailed keywords – and everything to do with completely empathizing with your reader and making him feel you and he are having a satisfying, helpful and enjoyable conversation. That's the real meaning of "killer content"!

Yes, by all means research keywords; but keep it simple, and don't waste time trying to be too foxy. Observe a few core rules and focus on writing articles and posts that really do give your readers the candy they've been craving in secret.

Conclude every post with a "call to action"; speak to them, not at them: in short, drive them naturally to your squeeze pages and sites. Don't forget to go for it with everything you've got.

Never, ever apologize, or cringe away from presenting that offer. As long as you're matching the perfect product with the right person, they're going to perceive that you did them an enormous, personal favor – and you're headed straight down the right highway towards Success!

Chapter 6 - Setting Goals and Having a Plan to Make More Money

Plans and goals go hand in hand, without one the other is redundant. Having both these elements highly featured in one's life is the key to keeping focused on gaining better life conditions every step into the future.

In most scenarios money play a big part in being the motivating factor that pushes the individual. The motivation levels of an individual are indeed what drive the endeavor to the success levels achieved.

As most people today are looking for easier ways to make money, the birth of many new endeavors are seems almost daily. More and more creative ways are being thought up with the main intention of making money as much and as quickly as possible.

The Passive Income Business for Starters

Once an individual has decided on a goal, the next step would be to come up with a suitable plan to execute the goal successfully. Points like marketability, commitment levels, financial investments, man power are just a few things that need to be considered when drawing up the plans.

Time frames are also another very important issue to consider when making plans towards reaching the goal. Most goals can be reached with a certain amount of commitment but in order to ensure the initial zest is not lost a suitable time frame must be put in place. This will not only ensure the goal is achieved but will also keep the individual focus on achieving it quickly. Taking the time to actually seriously consider the ambitions of the individual will help contribute to having a clearer picture of what the goals and plans should be. Indentifying this is most important to ensure the plan and goals are worked towards and finished successfully. Knowing one's capabilities and being realistic when deciding the goals and plans is also one way of being wise and prudent.

Those people who have successfully ventured into the passive income style of creating an income for them have been noted to have a very different mindset from the average individual.

These people are normally driven by ambition and money and will go to almost any lengths to achieve both. In the pursuit to achieving the desired residual income through passive means the individual needs to be willing to try any types of endeavors.

Generally the individual who chooses to provide residual incomes for themselves through the passive income style are people who are much focused and with a positive mindset. The strong positive mind set is almost a prerequisite in keeping the individual in track toward success.

Donnie Pratt
Being hopeful is also another attribute that is needed for this kind of endeavor. Because this style of residual income does not have the pressure on having to answer to superiors for not achieving a certain amount of business the individual has got to have the entire necessary positive attributes to be able to push themselves to the next level.

This is especially necessary when the energy levels are low and coupled with the fact that the perhaps there is a lack of visible achievements being evident.

Chapter 7 - Easy and Quick Ways to Make Money Online

Like a lot of other people on the Internet you may be looking for ways to supplement your income by making extra money online. However, your amount of available time may be limited due to your jobs, family or other responsibilities. In this article I'm going to share with you 10 quick and easy ways to make money online by spending just a few hours each week on your online business.

1. Make Money Online With a Video Sharing Site – With YouTube selling for $1.6 Billion it's no wonder that there are video sharing sites popping up all the time. Several versions of video sharing scripts are already available or you can get your own programmer to create a site to allow you to start your own video sharing site.

Rather than just creating more of the same you stand out from the crowd by creating a site for niche markets that would like to share videos. You could monetize your site with advertising that goes directly to the interest of your specific niche group.

2. Make Money Online With a Gaming Site – Online gaming is one of the hottest and most profitable niches online today. Millions of people of all ages love games of all sorts; not just sports or animated games. Some people like word and number games, strategic games like chess or even card games like Blackjack or Solitaire. There are affiliate programs and gaming site scripts available to help you capitalize on the online gaming frenzy.

3. Make Money Online Writing Articles – One of the most popular ways to make money online is by writing articles. With the high demand for original content in order to rank well on the major search engines, blog and website owners are willing to pay top dollars to good writers who can provide fresh articles on a regular basis. If you're a good writer then you may want to consider this lucrative income opportunity.

4. Make Money Online With a Niche Forum – Creating a niche forum is a great way to assemble a community of likeminded people. Niche forums appeal to thousands of people who want to network and socialize with other people who share their interests. As a forum owner you automatically have a mailing list that you can advertise to and have a great monthly income.

5. Make Money Online With Celebrity Blogs – It seems like now more than ever before we live in a celebrity driven culture. Pop stars have infiltrated even mainstream news channels and popular magazines. Celebrity culture represents a huge marketing opportunity that you can easily cash in on. You could set up a network of maybe five or six celebrity blogs with the latest information about your chosen celebrities. Link all of your blogs to each other to drive traffic to each one. You'll make money by monetizing your blogs with affiliate links that appeal to your audience.

6. Make Money Online as a Joint Venture Broker – A joint venture broker is an agent who brings product owners together with the right marketers with large lists to advertise the products to. The JV broker earns a percentage of the sales for making it all happen. Some internet marketers specialize in brokering these types of deals all the time and report earning very incomes by acting as the middleman in these ventures.

7. Make Money Online With a Local Tourist Site – If you live in or near a tourist area then this could be a great money making opportunity for you without requiring a big investment of your time. Just set up a simple website with information about your local area. Your site should make it easy for tourists to plan a trip to your area or find their way around once they arrive. Helpful features would be links to airports, hotels, restaurants, tourist attractions, and public transportation. You could make money from affiliate programs or from selling ad space to local businesses. These are all ways that can make a good income online without having to spend a lot of time or money to get started. Try any of these simple ideas to increase your cash flow without overloading your already busy schedule.

8. Make Money Online with Teleseminars & Webinars – Not very long ago only "big dogs" or major players online were able to conduct their own teleseminars or webinars. That's no longer the case and now a teleseminar or webinar is actually one of the most affordable products that you can create.

The easiest way to understand each of these is to remember that the root word is seminar. With either platform the basis is the information or seminar that is being presented. Otherwise, the difference is the way in which the seminar is delivered.

Of course, a teleseminar is conducted over the telephone; In fact, participating in a teleseminar sometimes feels like eavesdropping on a phone call between a guru and a student. A webinar is a seminar delivered over the internet or web using special software that allows you to make a presentation online and allows the audience to view the webinar on their computers.

9. Make Money Online with Audio eCourses – In today's fast paced world one of the things that you have to consider when creating products is how will your customer actually use the product. In many cases, your customer may like to download audio products to a computer or iPod to be able to listen to the content on the go.

You're probably familiar with ecourses. That's just a series of emails delivered via auto responder that gives you information on a particular subject. An audio ecourse would be very similar except your emails would include a link to an mp3 that the customer could download. They would then listen to the information rather than read an email.

Here are the four steps that you'll need to take in order to make money with audio ecourses:

> **1. Deciding on a topic** – You'll want to select a topic that you know for the start people will be interested in paying to learn more about. In order to do that just visit a few forums or groups within your niche and see what kind of questions are people asking repeatedly. When you've completed your ecourse you simply go back to these same forums or groups and let people know that you've got answers to their questions.
>
> **2. Creating content** – Once you decide on a topic you can either write the material yourself or purchase good quality PLR articles. Arrange the articles in a sequence that gives step-by-step instructions on how to complete the objective

or goal. You next need to record the lessons into downloadable MP3s.

3. Delivering the audio ecourse to your customers – Send customers to your sales page where you can tell them about the ecourse and pay. One they arrive at your download page they'll need to sign up through your auto responder system in order to receive the sequential emails.

As you can see, this is a very simple idea from start to finish. People will be willing to pay you because everyone loves convenience. One of the best ways to make money online or offline is by offering anything that makes life easier.

10. Make Money Online as a Coach/Consultant – The internet is the perfect place to grow your business as a coach or consultant in almost any field. The web gives you an opportunity to display your expertise in a variety of formats including writing, audio clips, or videos. All of these methods give you the opportunity to reach a global audience full of thousands of potential new clients. In return they all get a chance to "try out" your coaching or consultant style and level of expertise before they commit to a long term and possibly expensive contract.

Here are 5 ways that you can grow your business online as a coach or consultant:

1. Free or paid newsletters – A newsletter is a great way to introduce you to subscribers and give those helpful tips, information and strategies. You can even offer two subscription levels – a free subscription available to anyone and a paid model where you can give more thorough information to paid subscribers.

2. Articles – As a coach you can write articles that give specific information about the subjects or topics that interest your niche. Articles provide a quick way for readers to learn more about your way of thinking and develop the level of trust that you'll need to gain new customers.

3. EBooks – A further step from articles and special reports would be eBooks. This could allow you to go into more detail about what you offer as a coach or consultant. EBooks can be very resourceful because they save time so that you don't have to repeatedly go over the same information with multiple clients. For instance, if you are a marriage and relationship consultant there are some topics that are universal to all marriages. Instead of constantly saying the same thing to teach couple that you consult you can refer them to your eBook. At the same time you'll generate a new income stream.

4. Audio and Video Samples – Audios samples offer a good way to give instructions on certain topics and allow listeners to hear you and begin to bond with you is with the use of audio. These audio samples may include interviews, tips, podcasts or radio shows. Coaches that teach physical skills you may want to use videos to demonstrate the proper way to complete certain tasks. For example, it's much easier to teach someone how to paint a picture rather than write the instructions in an article or eBook. The visual aspect of some skills is very important to learning and video is a better format to present this type of training.

5. Teleseminars – One of the most popular marketing tools of coaches and consultants is the use of teleseminars. In as little as 45 minutes or less you can take a prospect from being completely unfamiliar with your product or service to someone who is totally convince that they MUST have you as a coach in order to survive. Teleseminars allow potential clients to learn all of the benefits of your service while investing nothing more than their time and attention.

11. Make Money Online as a Virtual Assistant – Do you have experience in the administrative field but don't want to return to the workplace right now? Maybe you're a new mother, are a college student, recently retired or recovering from an illness or operation. Here's how you can work at home and still earn a full time income. You can freelance from home using your skills as a Virtual Assistant. Virtual Assistance is one of the fastest growing industries on the internet. According to the George Washington University, it's expected to be a $130 billion industry by 2008.

These are a few of the tasks that virtual assistants perform:

- preparing documents

- managing databases

- making travel arrangements

- handling marketing projects

Virtual assistants also perform many other administrative tasks that are designed to increase productivity and decrease expenses.

12. Make Money Online Creating Your Own Software – This idea may seem intimidating at first...especially if you've never imagined yourself as a software creator. Heck, you might not even feel competent to operate most software, forget about creating it. You're not alone.

Let me assure you that you do not have to be a geek, a nerd, or even own a pair of suspenders in order to make money in the software business. The truth is that you don't have a clue about creating software in order to make money at it. You don't have to be the one who actual develops the software yourself. You can make money with software just by coming up with a great idea and hiring a programmer to make it happen.

13. Make Money Online with eBay Referrals – You probably already know at least a little something about making money by selling products on the world's largest marketplace – eBay. But did you know that you can make money without stocking, selling or shipping any merchandise at all. That's right. You can become an eBay affiliate and make money just by sending others to their website.

Go to eBay and join the affiliate program. The referral program is managed by Commission Junction and pays you a referral fee of $25 - $35 for everyone who makes a purchase within 30 days of clicking your link.

One good way to maximize your eBay referral income is to add eBay links and banners to your blog or website. Let your niche audience know how that they can find the items they're looking for on eBay and ask them to use your links. You can use eBay's flexible linking tool to send your customers directly to the page on eBay's site where they'll be sure to find the item that they're shopping for.

That's a win-win situation. Your customer will save time and effort in searching for the item and you'll earn a nice commission at the same time.

14. How to Make Money Online Selling Stock Photos – It seems like almost everywhere you look these days someone has a digital camera and is taking pictures nonstop. If you're one of those photo bugs who never get enough of taking pictures then a good way to turn your passion into profits is by becoming a stock photographer.

Stock photos are pictures that you allow a company to use for a commission. You may receive a flat fee per photo that is accepted or a commission on each download of your photo. Stock photography companies offer paid memberships to customers in the graphics or photography industry. Their membership fee allows them a certain number of credits that they may use to purchase the photos that they need for a particular project.

There are lots of stock photo companies around today such as:

√ iStockPhoto.com

√ BigStockPhoto.com

√ FotoSearch.com

√ SnapVillage.com

√ 123rf.com

You can take a look at each to determine which you prefer. When you know just what the designers are looking for you'll what photos to submit and get paid a lot more money.

15. Make Money Online with a Membership Site – One of the easiest ways to create a recurring income online is with a membership site. In fact, there's been a huge increase in the number of membership sites over the past few years. There are sites available for nearly every interest that you can imagine. Whether you're an animal lover, a work at home parent, a six figure earner, a music lover, or a sports fan there are membership sites for you.

But don't let the large number of sites already in existence intimidate you. Competition is a good thing. It lets you know that there are people willing to pay money for what you're thinking about doing.

To decide on a topic for your membership site just look at the latest trends going on in popular culture and the "evergreen" topics. Evergreens are those subjects that remain popular such as how to make money, how to have better relationships, weight loss, self improvement, sports and recreation, music, finances, home improvements, retirement, vacations and travel, electronics, etc. People are always interested in these subjects.

The best part of a membership site is that once you set up everything you can continue to make money each month without a lot of additional work. It only takes a few hours work to create new content and add it to your membership area. Plus it doesn't require a huge number of paying members for you to earn a good income. Look at this example:

If you make just $25 per member and you have a minimum of 500 members here's what your income could look like in just one year. I'll give you very modest numbers but you can always add new members each month and your income will continually grow.

The Passive Income Business for Starters
>25 X 500 = $12,500 per month X 12 months = $150,000 per year!

If you're thinking about starting your own membership site you'll need the software that allows you to set up a site automatically so that you don't have to handle issues like recurring billing, adding new members, cancelling subscribers, password problems and other technical concerns on your own.

Chapter 8 - Methods and Means for Passive Income Generation

Super Affiliate Marketer

Once you've built up your list with your passive income product, you can concentrate on becoming a super affiliate yourself.

Being a super affiliate is like any other job: You need to "practice" and stick with it until what is at first a struggle becomes an easy, familiar routine. (And – like any other 9-5 job you've worked at – it will become easy and familiar, if you just stick with it, and don't give up.)

On your way to being a super affiliate, you really can be making significant sums of income – perhaps even duplicating your monthly salary in a week – or a day – once your affiliate ball is rolling smoothly.

Driving Traffic to your Products

How you drive traffic to your products will differ – and make a big difference to how much passive income those products bring in.

Some top affiliate marketers never touch paid advertising, for example; others swear by it – even if they do it just long enough to kick-start new campaigns.

> **PPC** – Pay per Click ads are both a blessing and a curse. Why? Because you can't control how many people are going to click on your ad and actually visit your link to subscribe. You can't even control how many people are just going to click on your ad
>
> If lots subscribe, and several buy, it might be well worth the cost of the ads – but if everyone clicks and no one buys – that's a new marketer's worst nightmare. You're paying for every single one of those clicks.
>
> Fortunately, with most PPC networks, you can set a daily limit, and bid on lower-cost keywords that have enough traffic to be viable but not enough to be excessively expensive per click.
>
> You can also terminate the campaign, once the ball has started rolling and sales are coming in at a decent rate. Or you can keep it going, if you've determined – through tracking – that the Pay per Click ads are a major factor in those good monthly profits.

Keyword Research

It's a given that knowing how to do effective keyword research is one of the basics you should master straight away. So you may be wondering how the gurus and super affiliates do their keyword research.

While it's true that many do have favorite paid products. You'd be surprised how many super affiliates don't bother with paid programs, but keep their keyword research simple.

Donnie Pratt

One reason: they have focused so much on the lists they serve, they've developed a strong, natural feel for what's going to work and what is not. They've got an ear on the „net, and they know what trends are hot, what's evergreen, what problems their niche members are having their keyword research, and the long-tailed keywords they pick, are informed by all these factors.

Method # 1 - Access a free key words tool and type in your keyword. Pick likely long-tailed keywords (3 words or more) from the results. Check these phrases in Google's search box, contained in quotes. If there are a good number of searches, but these searches are still under 150,000, you've most likely got a viable niche to work

Method # 2 –Access a free key word tool and find some long-tailed keywords you think might be likely suspects. Go to Google Adwords KeyTool (it's free) and enter your phrases. Check the results (use "exact" mode, and focus only on monthly global search.). If the results for your phrase show some keyword competition (the little green "bars" are present and your results are over 1,000 in exact monthly global searches, go to Google. Check the phrase, in quotes, in their search box. If your results in Google Search still fit the under-150,000 criteria, you've got a winner!

The lower the number in Google, the better – but it should still have a good number of searches. The higher the number in Adwords, the better – but there's a point where Adwords competition is too strong.

Talk to your Niche

- Make it all about them

- Hang out on social media or forums where they do – and be the "solver", whenever someone's got a problem

The Passive Income Business for Starters
- Empathize with them, and get to know them. Be interested in their interests, and help them with their problems

Donnie Pratt
CPA Marketing

CPA, or cost-per-action marketing, is something you can add to your blogs – or get into, for its own sake.

The great thing about Cost Per Action is the "action" part: You get paid if people merely click on the link provided, because these links are strictly for lead generation.

Unless you know how to maximize CPA, however, you can end up putting a lot of work into something that brings you a downright small return. Here's what you need to know:

Some niches bring in significantly higher rewards, because they're funded by markets with huge budgets

- Some CPA networks are better than others

- Some CPA offers allow you not only to get paid for lead generation, but will pay commissions on actual sales, too – so it's worth your time to put a little more energy into promoting them.

- Some CPA networks also reward you for good sales. These are ones you'll be especially interested in, as a super affiliate.

Chapter 8- The Secret Methods of Using Passive Income Generators

The secret to Massive Passive income is to know WHERE to place your ads and how they should look in order to maximize clicks from your visitors. You must know how to do this without resorting to trickery or violating any section of your advertiser's agreement. This applies whether you are using Google, Yahoo or any of other advertisers you may choose to become associated with as a publisher!

So what can we do to make our ads more clickable? The first thing we need to do is make sure the ads "blend in" with our site page color schemes, overall page design and "flow" of the content. Secondly, we need to be sure the advertisements s will be seen by our visitors. If they cannot see them then obviously no manner what we do they want click on the ad – and no "Cha- Ch'ing". Doesn't that sound simple enough?

The actual appearance of your words is the most important factor. For example, here are some killers.

- Pages filed with typos

- Difficult to read or follow the text (odd fonts, a million links, multiple color fonts, black background, design in the background)

- BOLD and ALL CAPS FONTS everywhere on the page.

- Over-use of colors -- red is becoming the sign of an amateur. Save colors for very special circumstances.

A user-unfriendly site, with confusing and difficult navigation, is more deadly than not having your keywords in the top 1,000 search results. You may have the single most beautiful looking site overall but if you have one of those hierarchical, JavaScript-driven Navigation bars that folks can't figure out – you will lose business! It boils down to KISSM. Keep it Simple - Sell More!

Step back, every now and then, and ask yourself this all-important question. "Is this a look and feel that my visitors will like and actually use?" Obviously, it takes a very different approach to please the teen iPod lovers versus the quantum physicists versus the average adult surfer. Nevertheless, no manner whom your target is the value of good content will sink if its presentation – the look and usability (or feel) make it hard to navigate your site.

A good look and feel is dependent on overall page "flow" along with a simple navigation bar, or index. In order to accomplish the best "flow" you will need to build your pages in a defined hierarchal mode that makes sense. The secret is in the "tier structure" of your web pages.

The Passive Income Business for Starters

You may have more expertise and knowledge, in your chosen niche, than any of your competitors. However, if you cannot:·

• Get your messages across in a credible fashion

• Alternatively, if your visitors get lost trying to find their way around your site, it is all for naught.

Your visitors will not stick around long enough to see your strengths. On the other hand, a well-done look and feel will not complete your sale. Heck, it will not even complete the Pre-Selling. However, at least, a good look and feel will put your visitor on a good start. You will never earn commissions or generate sales on just the strength of your sites look and feel. But a bad look and feel will definitely kill you - no matter how well you do everything else.

A good solid look and feel simply sets the groundwork. It goes a long way to tuning in the subconscious mood, of your visitor, to receive your messages. At this point, your visitors are ready for you to deliver the information. They are also happy as they are able to move about your site smoothly, always securely aware of their location within your site. Therefore, now they are more than ready - they are subconsciously anxious, and open, to receive your Pre-sell message!

Chapter 9- What You Should Know About Online and Offline Business

1) There is no such thing as a Free Lunch. Yes, it will take some money to make money, the thing is being careful about what you spend. There are "gurus" who claim to know the secret to making money without doing any work or without spending any money. However those gurus expect you to spend $97 to buy their eBook in which they tell you how you can get people to buy the same eBook you just bought from them.

Once you get involved in a business, you will have to work. Even the programs that rave that you "don't have to do a thing" have but following that statement and that but is "...but advertise your website."

The Passive Income Business for Starters

Further this means that anyone who tells you building a business from home is easy and effortless is not being fully honest. But it can be fun, rewarding, fulfilling, and profitable with hard work and dedication.

2) You should always exercise leverage. Leverage is the ability to get people together to work for a common goal. When several people work together towards a common goal, it becomes much easier than with one person.

3) Rome was not built in a day. Sorry, Rome was not build in a day, and your business will not grow from nothing to hundreds in a week, a month. It will take time and work to build it into a business that will help you retire from that job that you hate, for whatever reason you dislike it.

Some people become "opportunity hoppers," and if an opportunity has not made them $$$$ in 3 weeks they move to the next. However this chronic jumping is about like planting and expecting to harvest the next week. Basically the opportunity hopper plants some corn, when a week later all it has done is show it's little green head. The jumper decides, "Well if that's all it's going to do, then I will just pull them up and plant tomatoes."

They will never really see the plants produce, because before the plants ever have time, the jumper is on something else. Most any company regardless of product, or compensation plan can succeed when you market it, talk to prospects, and take your time. Just like plants, if you do nothing, your business will not grow. And if you dig up your plants too soon, you will never see growth

4) If you want to replace your job, you must work this like a job. If you treat your business like your hobby, then do not be surprised when it grows very - very little and very - very slow. If you want it to replace your current job, then you must treat this like a job. You must decide to work it like a job.

Donnie Pratt

That means you spend time dedicated to marketing, talking to people doing what it takes to get the job done. Just like you would do whatever it takes to get your job done at your regular job. This is your future... your retirement, your ability to stay home with your family. It's how you decide when you want to take vacations. But you must work, to reach those goals you have long desired.

6) You should have Multiple Income Streams. Multiple Income Streams are like an insurance policy. If something happens to one income stream you have the others to help you maintain your income.

ABOUT THE AUTHOR

Donnie Pratt has worked for many of the large companies, in New Zealand and Australia, and is well versed in the language of investment. Now he works from home and earning from passive income online. His mission is to bring passive income knowledge to a wide range of people, not just those who already know the ins and outs of the market. He lives in Chicago.

www.ingramcontent.com/pod-product-compliance
Lightning Source LLC
LaVergne TN
LVHW010408260226
832611LV00016B/1382